What Is Regeneration?

Basics of the Faith

Sean Michael Lucas, Series Editor

What Is Regeneration?

Matthew Barrett

P&R
PUBLISHING
P.O. BOX 817 • PHILLIPSBURG • NEW JERSEY 08865-0817

Much of the material in this booklet is adapted from the author's book *Salvation by Grace: The Case for Effectual Calling and Regeneration* (Phillipsburg, NJ: P&R Publishing, 2013).

ISBN: 978-1-59638-659-4 (pbk)
ISBN: 978-1-59638-660-0 (ePub)
ISBN: 978-1-59638-661-7 (Mobi)

Page design by Tobias Design

Printed in the United States of America

Library of Congress Cataloging-in-Publication Data

Barrett, Matthew Michael, 1982-
  What is regeneration? / Matthew Barrett.
    pages cm. -- (Basics of the faith)
  Includes bibliographical references.
  ISBN 978-1-59638-659-4 (pbk.)
  1. Regeneration (Theology) I. Title.
  BT790.B37 2013
  234'.4--dc23

                    2013029807

THE BONDAGE OF THE WILL

"Because of the bondage of sin by which the will is held bound, it cannot move toward good, much less apply itself thereto; for a movement of this sort is the beginning of conversion to God, which in Scripture is ascribed entirely to God's grace."[1] These words, written by John Calvin, are a lethal blow to the common man's optimism concerning his spiritual ability in matters of salvation. Calvin's words, however, parallel what Scripture says.

Jesus himself states in John 8:34 that "everyone who commits sin is a slave to sin." Likewise, the apostle Paul tells us that man is dead in his trespasses and sins (Eph. 2:1) and that all of us are "by nature children of wrath" (Eph. 2:3). "The natural person," says Paul, "does not accept the things of the Spirit of God, for they are folly to him, and he is not able to understand them because they are spiritually discerned" (1 Cor. 2:14). As he says to the Corinthians, Paul also says to the Galatians, "In the same way we also, when we were children, were enslaved to the elementary principles of the world" (Gal. 4:3). And again, Paul explains to Timothy that prior to salvation the sinner is in the "snare of the devil, after being captured by him to do his will" (2 Tim. 2:26). Paul makes a similar statement in 2 Corinthians 4:4: "In their case the god of this world has blinded the minds of the unbelievers, to keep them from seeing the light of the gospel of the glory of Christ, who is the image of God."

In short, the sinner is very much like Lazarus, dead in the tomb, rotting away. As John Owen states, we have no more power than "a man in his grave hath in himself to live anew and come out at the next call."[2] Therefore, what the sinner needs is to hear the equivalent of the resurrection words of Christ: "Lazarus, come out" (John 11:43).

THE GOSPEL CALL AND THE EFFECTUAL CALL

But how exactly does God call sinners to himself and liberate them from their bondage to sin? According to Scripture, while God has a gospel call that goes out to all people, he also has an effectual call intended only for his elect.

The Gospel Call

Despite man's depravity, God is outrageously gracious to sinners, sending forth his gospel message to the ends of the earth, inviting and commanding sinners everywhere to repent and believe. The gospel call can be defined as the "offering of salvation in Christ to people, together with an invitation to accept Christ in repentance and faith, in order that they may receive the forgiveness of sins and eternal life."[3]

First, the gospel call is an invitation for everyone who hears the gospel. Hence, sometimes the gospel call is labeled the *general* or *universal* call, meaning that the gospel is preached indiscriminately to people of any age, race, or nation. As the Lord proclaims in Isaiah 45:22, "Turn to me and be saved, all the ends of the earth! For I am God, and there is no other" (cf. Isa. 55:1; John 4:10, 14; 6:35–51).

Second, the gospel call is a well-meant offer of salvation. The preaching of the gospel to all people comes out of a real, genuine desire to see all people repent and be saved

(Num. 23:19; Ps. 81:13–16; Prov. 1:24; Isa. 1:18–20; Ezek. 18:23, 32; 33:11; Matt. 21:37; 23:37; 1 Tim. 2:4; 2 Tim. 2:13; 2 Peter 2:9). Arminians often object that this cannot be the case if, as Calvinists believe, God chooses to give his effectual grace only to his elect. God's gospel offer would be disingenuous and cynical. However, there is no inconsistency for several reasons.

(1) Such an offer is not superfluous because the gospel call is the *very means* by which God converts sinners.

(2) God never makes a promise in the gospel offer that he does not keep. God promises that eternal life will be granted on the condition of faith. However, God never promises that he will bestow faith on everyone.

(3) The gospel call is seriously meant, regardless of the fact that man cannot fulfill it. It is put forth that since sinners do not have the ability to believe (due to depravity), a gospel call cannot be genuinely offered. However, man's inability to repent and believe is his own fault. God will not lower the conditions of the gospel (faith and repentance) because man, by his own depravity, cannot fulfill them. Moreover, God is not obligated to bestow his grace on anyone. Man is a sinner, deserving only judgment, and for God to fulfill the gospel condition on anyone's behalf is sheer grace.

Third, the gospel call is resistible. All those whom God has not elected will and do resist the gospel call and consequently further their condemnation before a holy God. One passage that makes such resistance especially evident is Acts 7, where

Stephen is martyred for his faith in Christ. Stephen gives a biblical theology of God's redemptive purpose through Israel, and when he comes to the end he reminds the Jews putting him on trial that they have failed to understand what the Scriptures have said concerning the "coming of the Righteous One" (7:52). Stephen accuses them of being just like their fathers who persecuted the prophets. "You stiff-necked people, uncircumcised in heart and ears, you always resist the Holy Spirit. As your fathers did, so do you" (Acts 7:51; cf. Heb. 3:8–13).

The resistibility of the gospel call is important to reiterate because often it is assumed that Calvinists deny the resistibility of grace. However, Calvinists affirm that God's grace *in the gospel call* can be resisted. It is *when God chooses to effectually call his elect* that such a calling cannot be finally resisted, for God's purpose in saving his elect will be accomplished without fail. The difference here is in God's intention and design. As John Owen says, "Where any work of grace is not effectual, God never intended it should be so, nor did put forth that power of grace which was necessary to make it so."[4]

The Effectual Call

When the gospel call is heard, why is it that some believe while others do not? In short, the reason for belief is not to be found in man's will but in God's effectual grace. Scripture teaches that when the gospel call goes out to all people, God secretly, irresistibly, and effectually calls his elect and only his elect to himself.

Scripture is replete with references to the effectual call. First, consider how effectual calling is spoken of by Paul.

When Paul refers to calling he is not referring to a gospel call, which is a mere invitation that can be resisted, but rather he is referring to that calling which is effective, performing and fulfilling exactly what it was intended to accomplish. We read in Romans 8:28–30,

> And we know that for those who love God all things work together for good, for those who are called according to his purpose. For those whom he foreknew he also predestined to be conformed to the image of his Son, in order that he might be the firstborn among many brothers. And those whom he predestined he also called, and those whom he called he also justified, and those whom he justified he also glorified.

Notice that Paul has the same exact group of people in mind throughout his entire chain of salvation, so that those predestined are the same ones who are called, and likewise those called are the same ones who are justified, etc. Therefore, calling necessarily proceeds from God's eternal election (cf. Rom. 9:11–12, 24–26; 1 Cor. 1:9; 2 Tim. 1:9; 1 Thess. 5:23–24; 2 Thess. 2:13–14). And Paul must be referring to a calling other than the gospel call, because in the gospel call it is not true that all those called are justified. Indeed, many disbelieve the gospel call and are never justified. Paul does not say that out of all those whom God calls some are justified and then glorified. No, Paul is clear: those whom God calls are indeed justified and also glorified. Therefore, since many reject the gospel call and are not justified, let alone glorified, Paul must be referring to a calling that unfailingly and immutably leads to and results in justification. It is this effectual call that is grounded in predestination and results in justification.

Moreover, Paul cannot have in mind here the gospel call because those who are "called" are promised that not only will all things work together for their good, but also they will be glorified (8:30), demonstrating that calling produces perseverance. Paul in verse 28 shows that the called he has in mind are only those who love God. These are "called according to his purpose," predestined, and promised that all things work together for good. Now it is true that the gospel call is also a call that is "according to his purpose," but it is not true that the gospel call is for only those who love God and those for whom all things work together for good. Therefore, Paul is referring to a call that works (cf. Rom. 1:6–7; 9:22–24).

Paul's use of the doctrine of the effectual call is also apparent in 1 Corinthians 1:18–31. The gospel Paul preached (the "word of the cross" in verse 18) is both the power and wisdom of God to those who are saved (1:18, 21, 24; cf. Rom. 1:16) and at the same time a gospel that is foolishness to those who disbelieve and perish (1:18, 23, 25). Notice that there is no change in the gospel. The gospel remains the same. However, some hear this gospel and see it as folly while others hear this gospel and see it as the power of life. Paul's words here are similar to those in 2 Corinthians 2:15–16, where the gospel is a fragrance of Christ. To those being saved it is an aroma of eternal life, but to those perishing it is an aroma of eternal death (2:15–16).

So if it is not the gospel itself that makes the difference, then what is it that accounts for the fact that some reject the gospel and see it as folly while others, who hear the same message of Christ crucified, accept the gospel as life? The answer is found in 1 Corinthians 1:23–24.

> But we preach Christ crucified, a stumbling block to Jews and folly to Gentiles, but to those who are called, both Jews and Greeks, Christ the power of God and the wisdom of God.

This specific group (the "called" ones) is in contrast to the larger group of Jews and Greeks whom Paul says received the message of Christ crucified and saw it as a stumbling block (Jews) and as folly (Gentiles). Such a contrast precludes any idea that Paul is referring only to a general gospel call. Moreover, Paul must have in mind a calling that is irresistible, because those identified as "the called" believe as a result of being called. In contrast to those who are not "the called" and therefore can only see the cross as folly, those who are identified as "the called" (both Jews and Greeks) consequently see Christ as the power and wisdom of God. Being called inevitably results in submitting to the lordship of Christ.

Furthermore, verses 26–31 preclude an Arminian interpretation, which would view the free will of the sinner as the basis for the success of God's call. Paul explains that those who are called are not chosen because of anything in them—their own wisdom or power, for example. How could this be when God purposefully chose those who were weak, lowly, and despised, "so that no human being might boast in the presence of God" (1:29)? If it were the case that certain Jews and Gentiles were called and regenerated because they themselves believed, then Paul could not exclude all boasting. Man would then have something to boast about "in the presence of God" (1:29). Rather, it is "because of him you are in Christ Jesus," and therefore if anyone is to boast he is to "boast in the Lord" (1:31).

Many other passages speak of an effectual call (1 Cor. 7:15; Gal. 1:15–16; 5:13; Eph. 4:1–6; Col. 3:15; 1 Thess. 4:7; 1 Tim. 6:12; 2 Tim. 1:9; 1 Peter 1:14–15; 2:9–10, 21; 2:21; 3:9; 5:10; 2 Peter 1:3–5, 10; Jude 1:1–2; Rev. 17:14). However, no one so strongly emphasizes the effectual nature of calling as Jesus does in John 6:35–44. Why is it that some see the signs and hear the message of Jesus and believe while others, seeing the very same signs and hearing the very same message, disbelieve? What is to account for belief and unbelief? Notice that Jesus does not explain why some believe and others do not by saying that some choose him while others do not. While he holds out the promise of life to all (6:35–37, 40, 47, 51), he never says that everyone has the spiritual ability to believe, nor does he attribute belief to man's free will. On the contrary, Jesus highlights the inability of man when he says, "No one can come to me unless the Father who sent me draws him" (v. 44).

What determines whether people will come to Jesus, then, is whether or not the Father has chosen to give them to his Son. As we read in verse 37, "All that the Father gives me will come to me." Jesus places the decisive factor in the will of the Father, not in the will of man.

This brings us to the precise nature of such a drawing in John 6:37, 44, and 65. These three passages read,

> All that the Father gives me will come to me, and whoever comes to me I will never cast out. (John 6:37)

No one can come to me unless the Father who sent me draws him. And I will raise him up on the last day. (John 6:44)

And he said, "This is why I told you that no one can come to me unless it is granted him by the Father." (John 6:65)

Is such a drawing effectual and irresistible? Or, as the Arminian believes, can this drawing be resisted successfully? Jesus teaches that the grace of which he is speaking here is one that is particular to the elect and effectual. Several observations bear this out. In John 6, especially verse 44, the drawing of the Father necessarily results in a coming to Christ. In other words, this is not a drawing that merely makes possible a coming to Christ, but rather is a drawing that inevitably and irresistibly leads to Christ. All those drawn do in fact believe. As Jesus explains in 6:44, "No one can come to me unless the Father who sent me draws him. And I will raise him up on the last day." Arminians view 6:44 as saying that while it is true that no one can come to Christ unless the Father draws him, such a drawing can be resisted. However, such an interpretation fails in two ways: it ignores the fact that "no one can come to me" (i.e., inability) and it fails to finish the verse: "I will raise him up on the last day." Each of these points deserves consideration.

First, in John 6 the grammatical language is in support of an irresistible, effectual drawing. The word *draw* in Greek is *elkō*, which, as Albrecht Oepke explains, means "to compel by irresistible superiority."[5] Though the Arminian rejects such a notion, the word linguistically and lexicographically means "to compel." Therefore, Jesus cannot be saying that the drawing of the Father is a mere wooing or persuasion that can be resisted. Rather, this drawing is an indefectible, invincible, unconquerable, indomitable, insuperable, and unassailable summons. In short, this summons does not fail to accomplish what God intended.

Second, the Father's drawing will indeed result in final salvation, the resurrection on the last day, as is evident in John 6:44. Jesus comes down from heaven to do the will of the Father, and what is this will but to lose none of all those whom the Father has given to him and to raise them up on the last day (John 6:39–40)? In other words, Jesus is referring only to those whom the Father has given him—to these only will Jesus give eternal life and the resurrection to glory. Here we see once again that the Father's giving of the elect to the Son unfailingly leads to final salvation. Therefore, the drawing Jesus speaks of must be effectual.

REGENERATION

A discussion of regeneration flows naturally from effectual calling. Those whom God effectually calls to himself are made alive (Rom. 8:7–8; Eph. 2:1, 5; Col. 2:13). The actual word *regeneration* (*palingenesia*) is used only in Matthew 19:28 (NASB, KJV) and Titus 3:5, and only the latter uses the word in the narrow sense, namely, as referring to the first instance of new life. Nevertheless, the *concept* of regeneration in this narrow sense is affirmed throughout Scripture, for even if the word itself is not used, the idea is prevalent. That said, it is appropriate to precisely define regeneration in this narrow sense.

Regeneration is the work of the Holy Spirit to unite the elect sinner to Christ by breathing new life into that dead and depraved sinner so as to raise him from spiritual death to spiritual life, removing his heart of stone and giving him a heart of flesh, so that he is washed, born from above and now able to repent and trust in Christ as a new creation. Moreover, regeneration is the act of God alone and therefore it is monergistic in nature, accomplished by the sovereign act of the Spirit apart from and unconditioned upon man's will to believe. In short, man's faith does not cause regeneration but regeneration causes man's faith.[6]

With this definition in view, let's now look to Scripture itself, particularly with the monergistic nature of regeneration in mind.

The Circumcision and Gift of a New Heart

Deuteronomy 30:6. In Deuteronomy 30 Israel faces and anticipates the reality of coming exile and judgment for disobedience. However, Moses foretells of a time to come when Israel will experience restoration, redemption, genuine repentance, and new spiritual life rather than judgment and condemnation. Included in such a future restoration is liberation from the slavery of sin. However, liberation from bondage to sin comes only through the circumcision of the heart (i.e., regeneration). In Deuteronomy 30:6 we read, "And the LORD your God will circumcise your heart and the heart of your offspring, so that you will love the LORD your God with all your heart and with all your soul, that you may live."

If the circumcision of the heart refers to regeneration (cf. Rom. 2:25–27), then to what purpose does God promise to circumcise the heart? He circumcises the heart "so that" his people will love the Lord. The Lord does not circumcise their hearts "because" they acted in repentance and faith by loving the Lord. Rather, it is God's sovereign act of circumcising the heart that causes the sinner to love him. Nowhere in Deuteronomy 30:6 do we see any indication that God's sovereign act of circumcising the heart is conditioned on the will of man to believe. Rather, it is quite the opposite. The Lord must first circumcise the heart so that the sinner can exercise a will that believes.

In Deuteronomy 29:2–4 Moses summons all of Israel and says,

> You have seen all that the LORD did before your eyes in the land of Egypt, to Pharaoh and to all his servants and to all his land, the great trials that your eyes saw, the signs, and those great wonders. But to this day the LORD has not given you a heart to understand or eyes to see or ears to hear.

Why is it that those in Israel, who saw the many miracles God performed in saving them from Pharaoh, do not believe? Verse 4 gives the answer: "To this day the LORD has not given you a heart to understand or eyes to see or ears to hear." It is remarkable how much Deuteronomy 29 parallels John 10:26. As Israel saw the miracles and failed to hear and see spiritually, so also did the Jews in the Gospels see the miracles of Jesus and fail to hear and see spiritually. But again, notice the reason Jesus gives as to why they do not believe,

The works that I do in my Father's name bear witness about me, but you do not believe because you are not part of my flock. (John 10:25–26)

As in Deuteronomy 29:2–4, the reason they do not see or hear is because God did not give them "a heart to understand or eyes to·see or ears to hear." It is not man's choice or will that determines whether he will spiritually have a heart to hear and see; it is God's sovereign choice to give the sinner a heart to hear and see that is the cause and reason for belief.

Jeremiah 31:33 and 32:39–40. The concept of a new heart is also illustrated by the prophet Jeremiah. "For this is the covenant that I will make with the house of Israel after those days, declares the LORD: I will put my law within them, and I will write it on their hearts. And I will be their God, and they shall be my people" (Jer. 31:33; cf. Heb. 8:10; 10:16). Similarly the Lord says in Jeremiah 32:39–40,

I will give them one heart and one way, that they may fear me forever, for their own good and the good of their children after them. I will make with them an everlasting covenant, that I will not turn away from doing good to them. And I will put the fear of me in their hearts, that they may not turn from me.

Unlike in Deuteronomy 30:6 (NIV), in Jeremiah the phrase "circumcise your hearts" is not used. Nevertheless, the phrase is used in Jeremiah 4:4 (NIV) and the concept is present in Deuteronomy 30:6 and 32:39–40, for the text does speak of the Lord writing his law on the hearts of his people (in contrast to writing his law on tablets of stone), giving his people one heart, and putting the fear of the Lord in their hearts. As in Deuteronomy, in Jeremiah regeneration is in view. Notice that given the spiritual inability of the people (see Jer. 6:10), it is only when God writes his law within, on the heart, and places a fear of himself within that the sinner can follow after him.

Ezekiel 11:19–21 and 36:26–27. The concept of a circumcised heart in Deuteronomy 30:6 and a new heart in Jeremiah 31:33 is also taught in Ezekiel 11:19–21 and 36:26–27. God again promises a day to come when his people will experience restoration and renewal. He explains that in order for a sinner to walk in his statutes, keep his rules, and obey his law, God himself must first remove the dead, cold, lifeless heart of stone and replace it with a heart that is alive, namely, a heart of flesh. The Lord does not give the sinner a heart of flesh because the sinner obeys, but rather the sinner obeys *because* the Lord surgically implants a heart of flesh. Such an order is indicated at the beginning of 11:20. God removes the heart of stone and gives his people a heart of flesh that they may obey (11:21; 36:27). The same causal order is even more apparent in Ezekiel 36, where the Lord states that he will "cause you to walk in my statutes and be careful to obey my rules" (36:27). Once again, God does not put a new heart and spirit within in reaction to or because of the sinner's faith, but it is God's sovereign act of implanting a new heart, a new spirit, that causes the sinner to turn in faith and obedience (cf. Ezek. 37:1–14).[7]

The New Birth

John 3:3–8. Perhaps one of the most well-known and important texts on the new birth or regeneration is the encounter

Jesus has with Nicodemus. Nicodemus begins the dialogue by stating, "Rabbi, we know that you are a teacher come from God, for no one can do these signs that you do unless God is with him" (3:2). It may appear that Jesus avoids answering the assertion made by Nicodemus when he responds, "Truly truly, I say to you, unless one is born again he cannot see the kingdom of God" (3:3). However, Jesus is simply getting to the heart of the matter, directing Nicodemus's attention to how it is that one can know God in a saving way. Nicodemus seems to be implying a question to which he is hoping for an answer—namely the question, who are you, Jesus?

The answer Jesus gives shows that the only way one can truly know who God is (and therefore who Jesus claims to be) is by being born again (or "born from above"). In other words, Nicodemus will never believe Jesus is from God (let alone that Jesus is the Son of God) unless he first receives the new birth from the Spirit. Therefore, rather than telling Nicodemus, "Yes, I am from God," Jesus responds by saying that unless one is born by the Spirit he will never understand who Jesus is in a saving way. It is not by human reasoning but by spiritual rebirth that one comes to understand Jesus.

Moreover, Jesus is insistent that if Nicodemus is not born again he will not enter the kingdom of God. In theological language, Jesus is teaching the necessity of the new birth. The necessity of this new birth leads Jesus also to explain in 3:5–6 exactly what it means to be born again.

> Truly, truly, I say to you, unless one is born of water and the Spirit, he cannot enter the kingdom of God. That which is born of the flesh is flesh, and that which is born of the Spirit is spirit.

Jesus says that the birth he speaks of is one not of flesh but of the Spirit (v. 6). If one is born of the Spirit he is spirit. Jesus' use of *flesh* (*sarx*) here is not the same as Paul's use of *flesh*, where *flesh* refers to the sinful, enslaved nature. Rather, Jesus is referring to flesh as physical flesh. In other words, the contrast is not between sinful flesh and spiritual new life but between physical birth and spiritual birth or new life. Hence, Nicodemus misunderstands the words of Jesus as referring to physical birth. Jesus must clarify for Nicodemus—and for us—that he is talking not about an earthly birth of human flesh, but about a spiritual birth from above.

Furthermore, this second birth is of "water and the Spirit" (3:5). The best interpretation of "water" is one that identifies water symbolically. Water is used to represent the spiritual washing that must take place for one to be regenerated. Such an association of water with cleansing is supported in the Old Testament. As already seen, God promised in Ezekiel 36:25–27,

> I will sprinkle clean water on you, and you shall be clean from all your uncleannesses, and from all your idols I will cleanse you. And I will give you a new heart, and a new spirit I will put within you. And I will remove the heart of stone from your flesh and give you a heart of flesh. And I will put my Spirit within you, and cause you to walk in my statutes and be careful to obey my rules.

Water then coordinates with the Spirit, demonstrating the cleansing, purifying nature of the Holy Spirit in regeneration (cf. 3:6). Such a washing or cleansing is at the very essence of what it means to be born by the Spirit.

Before we move on to John 3:7–8, it is essential to observe that the language of "birth" in John 3:3–7 precludes the possibility of synergism. The miracle of human birth is a unilateral activity. There is nothing the infant does to be born. The infant does not birth himself. Nor is it the case that birth is conditioned on the infant's will to accept it or not. Likewise, the same is true with spiritual birth. Man is dead in his sins and spiritually in bondage to sin. His only hope is the new birth, and yet such a birth is a unilateral, monergistic act of God. Man plays no role whatsoever in the spiritual birthing event. Rather, God acts alone to awaken new life, as demonstrated in the use of the *passive voice*, which tells the reader that the recipient of this new birth is absolutely inactive. Jesus is emphasizing, through the image of birth, the passivity and inability of the sinner and the autonomy of God in creating new life. This same principle of monergism is taught again by Jesus as he further explains the role of the Spirit in John 3:7–8.

Already Jesus has indicated that one must be born of water and Spirit (John 3:5), demonstrating that the new birth is effected by the power of the Spirit. But two other points demonstrate the sovereignty of the Spirit as well. First, the sovereignty of the Spirit is demonstrated by both the presence of the divine passive and the emphasis Jesus places on human inability in John 3:3–8. The Spirit is the one who causes sinners to experience this new birth from above. Second, the sovereignty of the Spirit is manifested in how Jesus compares the Spirit to the wind. Jesus states,

> Do not marvel that I said to you, "You [plural] must be born again." The wind [spirit] blows where it wishes, and you hear its sound, but you do not know where it

comes from or where it goes. So it is with everyone
who is born of the Spirit. (John 3:7–8)

In the Greek the word for *spirit* (*pneuma*) is also "wind," and
likewise the word for *wind* is also "spirit." Jesus is drawing a clear
parallel here between wind and Spirit (as made obvious by 3:8),
so that when he speaks of one he is speaking of the other. He is
comparing the effects of the wind to the effects of the Spirit. It
is very important to note that the phrase "the wind blows where
it wishes" conveys the sovereignty of the Spirit. The Spirit is
not controlled by the human will; he works when and where
God pleases to bring about new life. Therefore, a regeneration
dependent on man's will to believe or a regeneration in which
God and man cooperate is ruled out by this text.

  1 John 5:1. Just as the gospel of John teaches that the grace
that regenerates is monergistic, preceding man's faith, the same
truth is evident in John's first epistle. For example, consider
1 John 5:1: "Everyone who believes that Jesus is the Christ *has
been* born of God, and everyone who loves the Father loves who-
ever has been born of him." Notice that *believes* in the phrase
"Everyone who believes" (or "Everyone believing") is a present
active participle in the nominative case, indicating ongoing
faith. In contrast, when John says that all those believing "*have
been* born of him," "have been born" is a perfect passive indicative, meaning that it is an action that has already taken place in
the past (it is completed) and has ongoing effects in the present.
In 1 John 5:1, in other words, the action in the perfect passive
indicative (regeneration) precedes and causes the action in the
present active participle (faith). The result is clear: God's act
of regeneration precedes belief. The implication, therefore, is

that it is God's act of regeneration that creates the faith man needs to believe.

The use of the perfect in 1 John 5:1 can also be found in 1 John 2:29, 3:9, 4:7, and 5:4, 18. In these texts we likewise learn that being righteous (2:29), resisting sin (3:9), loving God and neighbor (4:7), having saving knowledge of God (4:7 and 5:1), possessing a faith that overcomes the world (5:4), and abstaining from sin (5:18) all result from and are caused by regeneration.

But what about John 1:12–13, which reads,

> But to all who did receive him, who believed in his name, he gave the right to become children of God, who were born, not of blood nor of the will of the flesh nor of the will of man, but of God.

Does this text not teach that believing (faith) brings about becoming children of God (the new birth)? John 1:12–13 actually proves the exact opposite.

First, it is mistaken to assume that the phrase "become children of God" is synonymous with "new birth." Why should the reader assume that the phrase "become children of God" is synonymous with the new birth? Why not interpret becoming a child of God as the result of the new birth? Why not interpret such a phrase as referring to adoption, which is produced by the new birth? Indeed, there are several reasons why the phrase "become children of God" is referring to adoption, not regeneration.

(1) The phrase "children of God" in John 1:12 is also used by Paul in Romans 8:15–16 to refer to adoption, not regeneration. Paul writes,

> For you did not receive the spirit of slavery to fall
> back into fear, but you have received the Spirit of
> adoption as sons, by whom we cry, "Abba! Father!"
> The Spirit himself bears witness with our spirit that
> we are children of God. (Rom. 8:15–16; cf. Eph. 1:5)

Paul's language of adoption is reiterated when he says
in Galatians 3:26, "For in Christ Jesus you are all sons
of God, through faith" (cf. Gal. 4:5). As a consequence
to believing (John 1:12) or having faith (Gal. 3:26), one
is adopted into God's family as a son.

(2) Adoption is emptied of meaning if it is the case that
regeneration refers to already being placed in God's
family, receiving all the privileges of an heir.

Second, in order to argue that the phrase "become children of God" is referring to the new birth or regeneration, one
must take a leap that is not warranted by the text and assume
the text reads that one becomes a child of God because one
believes. However, the text does not make such a causal cor-
relation in 1:12. In fact, causal language does not come into
view until verse 13, which actually prohibits the new birth
from being conditioned on man's free will and brings us to
the third problem.

Third, we cannot ignore verse 13, which reads, "who
were born, not of blood nor of the will of the flesh nor of the
will of man, but of God." Verse 13 actually clarifies and quali-
fies verse 12. In other words, being born is in no way due to
"the will of man." Since the will of man is involved in faith,
there is no way that faith could precede being born again.

To conclude verse 13, John makes it clear that the new birth is *not* conditioned on man's will but is completely and only the act of God. Therefore, we cannot conclude from verse 12 that regeneration is conditioned on man's faith.

Brought Forth by God's Will: James 1:18

James also has much to say concerning regeneration: "Of his own will he brought us forth by the word of truth, that we should be a kind of firstfruits of his creatures" (James 1:18). It is important to note two things in this passage. First, "brought us forth" refers to regeneration, as it is a metaphor for spiritual rebirth. As seen with John 3, just as a baby is brought forth or birthed from the womb, so the sinner is brought forth or birthed by the power of God.

Second, God brought us forth of "his own will." The emphatic *his* highlights both the gracious benevolence of God in begetting new life to sinners and the omnipotence of God in doing so by "his own will." James' language here is very similar to Peter's when he says that according to God's mercy "he has caused us to be born again" (1 Peter 1:3). James also shares similarities with John, who states that those who believe are born not of the will of man but of God (John 1:12–13). Again, no mention is made of man's cooperation with God's grace, nor is there any hint by James that God's work of bringing us forth is conditioned on man's will to believe. On the contrary, James places all the emphasis on God. It is God's will, not man's, that brings the sinner into new life in order that he should be the firstfruits of God's creatures. Therefore, it is "by His doing you are in Christ Jesus" (1 Cor 1:30 NASB).

Caused to be Born Again: 1 Peter 1:3–5

Peter also emphasizes God's sovereignty in the new birth.

> Blessed be the God and Father of our Lord Jesus Christ!
> According to his great mercy, he has caused us to be
> born again to a living hope through the resurrection
> of Jesus Christ from the dead, to an inheritance that is
> imperishable, undefiled, and unfading, kept in heaven
> for you, who by God's power are being guarded through
> faith for a salvation ready to be revealed in the last
> time. (1 Peter 1:3–5)

Peter uses the language of causation to describe God's merciful yet powerful act of new birth. Several observations are necessary.

First, the reason Peter gives as to why God is to be praised is that in his great mercy God caused us to be born again. Peter will use the language of spiritual begetting again in 1 Peter 1:23, where he says that they "have been born again, not of perishable seed but of imperishable, through the living and abiding word of God." Here Peter shows that God the Father takes the initiative in producing spiritual children by his Word.

Second, Peter says that this new birth is according to God's great mercy. By definition mercy precludes any possibility of human works or contribution. Sinners prior to the new birth are dead in sin and deserving only of God's judgment and wrath. However, as will be seen in Ephesians 2:4–5, God granted mercy to those who rebelled against him.

Third, the image of birth is used and, as in John 3:5–6, so also in 1 Peter 1:3–5 such an image precludes any human contribution. This becomes apparent when Peter states that out of this great mercy God *caused* us to be born again. God causes, creates, brings about, and produces the new birth not on the basis of anything we have done but purely on the basis of his great mercy.

Made Alive with Christ

Ephesians 2:1–7. While Jesus and Peter explain regeneration through the imagery of birth, Paul explains regeneration through the imagery of resurrection from the dead.

> And you were dead in the trespasses and sins in which you once walked, following the course of this world, following the prince of the power of the air, the spirit that is now at work in the sons of disobedience—among whom we all once lived in the passions of our flesh, carrying out the desires of the body and the mind, and were by nature children of wrath, like the rest of mankind. But God, being rich in mercy, because of the great love with which he loved us, even when we were dead in our trespasses, made us alive together with Christ—by grace you have been saved—and raised us up with him and seated us with him in the heavenly places in Christ Jesus, so that in the coming ages he might show the immeasurable riches of his grace in kindness toward us in Christ Jesus. (Eph. 2:1–7)

In Ephesians 2 we see a powerful picture of what takes place in regeneration. The sinner is dead, but God makes him alive. The sinner is in the grave, but God resurrects him from the dead. Notice that, contrary to Arminianism, there is no contingency here or intermediate stage in which God begins to make a sinner alive but is dependent on the sinner's decision in order to finish. Rather, the transition is immediate, instantaneous, and unilateral as the sinner is at one moment dead and the next moment alive (Eph. 2:10). The situation is comparable with the resurrection of Christ. Christ was dead, but God in great power resurrected him bodily from the grave (Eph. 1:19–20). Or consider Lazarus, who was dead, rotting in the tomb for days, and suddenly, at the command of Christ, he was resurrected and walked out of the tomb alive (John 11).

Moreover, not only does the sinner who is "made alive" have a situation comparable to Christ, but the new life he receives is actually found in and with Christ. Paul states that God made us alive *together with Christ* and seated us with Christ in the heavenly places (2:6), so that in the coming ages we would know the immeasurable riches of his grace in kindness toward us *in Christ Jesus* (2:7). We are right in identifying being made alive with the resurrection of Christ (1 Peter 1:3). It is Christ's resurrection that is the very basis of the sinner's coming to life with Christ, as is further demonstrated in 2:6, where the sinner is raised up and seated in Christ. Our spiritual resurrection to new life is made explicit by what Paul contrasts it to, namely, deadness in trespasses and sins and bondage to the world (2:1–2), Satan (2:2), and the flesh (2:3). Like the rest of mankind, we were "by nature children of wrath" (2:3). Therefore, being made alive implies not only forgiveness, but also liberation from our former slavery.

Finally, in verse 5 Paul also states that being made alive together with Christ is by grace ("by grace you have been saved"). As seen throughout Paul's epistles, grace stands opposed to merit or any contribution on the part of man (Eph. 2:8–10). Grace is God's favor toward sinners in spite of what they deserve (Rom. 3:21–26; 4:4; 5:15). The word *save* can and is many times used to refer to an eschatological reality: deliverance from God's wrath and final judgment (1 Thess. 2:16; 1 Cor. 3:15; 5:5; 10:33; Rom. 5:9–10; 9:27; 10:9; 11:26). Moreover, in some passages Paul can also describe "saved" as an event in the present (1 Cor. 1:18; 15:2; 2 Cor. 2:15), so that he can even say, "Now is the day of salvation" (2 Cor. 6:2; cf. Isa. 39:8).

However, the case differs in Ephesians 2, for *saved* refers specifically to what has already taken place and been accomplished in the past. In other words, Paul is referring to salvation as something that is already present for Christians. Yes, Paul does draw our attention to the future eschatological consequences of this salvation in verse 6 (being seated with Christ in the coming age). However, in verses 4–5 Paul shows that being saved by grace means that God's making us alive together with Christ is also by grace.

Therefore, being made alive or regenerated is neither an act that is accomplished by man's works-righteousness nor an act conditioned on man's willful cooperation. Rather, being made alive is *by grace and by grace alone*, meaning that it is purely by God's initiative, prerogative, and power that the sinner is resurrected from spiritual death. Therefore, it will not do to say that God's grace is a gift to be accepted or resisted. Yes, God's grace is a gift, but more than that it is a powerful gift that actually and effectually accomplishes new life as God intends.

Colossians 2:11–14. Another passage of Scripture that is a powerful example of monergistic regeneration is Colossians 2:11–14, where Paul writes to the Colossians,

> In him [Christ] also you were circumcised with a
> circumcision made without [human] hands, by put-
> ting off the body of the flesh, by the circumcision of
> Christ, having been buried with him in baptism, in
> which you were also raised with him through faith in
> the powerful working of God, who raised him from
> the dead. And you, who were dead in your trespasses
> and the uncircumcision of your flesh, God made alive
> together with him, having forgiven us all our tres-
> passes, by canceling the record of debt that stood
> against us with its legal demands. This he set aside,
> nailing it to the cross.

In verse 11 Paul presents the metaphor of circumcision, a clear reference to the Old Testament when Moses and the prophets Jeremiah and Ezekiel called for a "circumcision of the heart" (Deut. 10:16; 30:6; Jer. 4:4; Ezek. 44:7; cf. Rom. 2:17). The contrast Paul makes, however, is not a circumcision by human hands but a circumcision by the Spirit on the heart that is needed for a person to experience new life in Christ.

As already seen, the metaphor of circumcision itself com-municates the monergistic work of God. Spiritual circumci-sion is an act performed on the recipient by God, apart from the sinner's cooperation. God and God alone circumcises the heart, and then and only then can the sinner trust in Christ. It is only when spiritual circumcision takes place that the sinner is set free from the flesh. As Paul states in verse 12, we have been "raised with him through faith in the powerful working of God, who raised him from the dead." Paul transitions from the metaphor of circumcision to the metaphor of resurrection. Notice the parallel Paul makes in verses 12–13 between God raising Christ from the dead and God spiritually raising the sinner from the dead. Paul calls this act the "powerful work of God," and rightly so, for just as God takes a dead body and brings it to life, so also does he take a dead soul and breathe new spiritual life into it.

The Washing of Regeneration: Titus 3:3–7

Paul's words in Colossians show many similarities to his words in Titus.

> For we ourselves were once foolish, disobedient, led astray, slaves to various passions and pleasures, passing our days in malice and envy, hated by others and hating one another. But when the goodness and loving kindness of God our Savior appeared, he saved us, not because of works done by us in righteousness, but according to his own mercy, by the washing of regeneration and renewal of the Holy Spirit, whom he poured out on us richly through Jesus Christ our Savior, so that being justified by his grace we might become heirs according to the hope of eternal life. (Titus 3:3–7)

As in Ephesians 2 and Colossians 2, Paul begins in Titus 3 with man's depravity and slavery to sin, once again emphasizing man's deadness to sin and his spiritual inability. Prior to the washing of regeneration, man was a slave to evil desires (cf. Titus 2:12; 1 Tim. 6:9), spending his time in malice, envy, and hatred. However, out of his love and goodness "God our Savior" saved us. How exactly did he save us? Not by our own works of righteousness but purely according to his "own mercy." Therefore, according to Paul, salvation is unconditional. Such mercy is made effective by the power of the Holy Spirit, who washes the sinner clean, as Paul says, "by the washing of regeneration and renewal of the Holy Spirit" (3:5; cf. 2:14). The very purpose of Christ's redeeming work is for the Spirit to purify a people unto God.

Two observations can be made. First, Paul's two prepositional phrases provide the basis for God's redemption of sinners, the first of which dismisses any human contribution and the second of which is a very strong affirmation of salvation based completely on God's mercy. Therefore, works-righteousness or works plus faith is clearly eliminated by Paul. Second, one does not escape the unconditionality of this passage by arguing that while one is saved by faith alone, not works, one must cooperate with God's grace in order to receive the washing of regeneration. This is the Arminian argument, and it still contradicts the point Paul is making—namely, that man can contribute absolutely nothing whatsoever to God's work, including the washing of regeneration.

Contrary to the Arminian argument, man is passive in the washing of regeneration. Such a point is further proven by the language Paul uses for regeneration. Paul refers to regeneration as a "washing" that is accomplished by the Spirit who renews. Paul's language here parallels 1 Corinthians 6:11, where he begins with a long list of the types of depravity the believer once walked in but then says, "Such were some of you. But you were washed, you were sanctified, you were justified in the name of the Lord Jesus Christ and by the Spirit of our God." Notice that not only does Paul use the same metaphor of being "washed" to refer to the change and inner renewal or cleansing that must take place, but he once again ties the washing of regeneration to the agency of the Spirit.

Paul's union of regeneration and Spirit both in Titus 3:3–7 and in 1 Corinthians 6:11 uses the Old Testament language of Ezekiel 36:25–27: "I will sprinkle clean water on you, and you shall be clean from all your uncleannesses, and from all your idols I will cleanse you" (36:25). God, through Ezekiel, goes on to say in 36:26–27 that he will give his people a new heart, putting his Spirit within, and will cause them to walk in his ways. Paul, like Ezekiel, is emphasizing the power of the Spirit to wash or regenerate the sinner, causing him to walk in obedience and new life.

As already demonstrated, Ezekiel 36 and John 3 both attribute to the Spirit the sovereign work of regeneration, which is always monergistic. Paul is no different. As demonstrated already in Ephesians 2:5 and Colossians 2:11–14, so also in Titus 3 Paul connects the washing of regeneration with the Spirit, who, like the wind, blows wherever he wills, quickening sinners from death to new life. The difference in Titus 3 is that the metaphor has changed slightly from regeneration as birth (John 3:5) or the resurrection from death to new life (Eph. 2:5; Col. 2:13) or circumcision (Col. 2:13), to the washing of the dirty and stained sinner. Though the metaphor shifts, the message remains the same.

Let Light Shine out of Darkness: 2 Corinthians 4:3–6

A final passage that serves to complement what has been seen so far is 2 Corinthians 4:3–6, where we read that God has shone in the hearts of sinners "to give the light of the knowledge of the glory of God in the face of Jesus Christ" (v. 6). Here we see an example of the revealing of the Son to those who are veiled and blinded. However, it is not a mere revelation that takes place; the knowledge Paul speaks of is actually a "light" that pierces into the heart and, as in the process of creation, brings into existence a heart that has been radically changed. To understand this miracle we need to look at the entire passage.

> And even if our gospel is veiled, it is veiled only to those who are perishing. In their case the god of this world has blinded the minds of the unbelievers, to keep them from seeing the light of the gospel of the glory of Christ, who is the image of God. For what we proclaim is not ourselves, but Jesus Christ as Lord, with ourselves as your servants for Jesus' sake. For God, who said, "Let light shine out of darkness," has shone in our hearts to give the light of the knowledge of the glory of God in the face of Jesus Christ. (2 Cor. 4:3–6)

The unbeliever is veiled to the truth of the gospel, blinded by the god of the world so that he cannot see the light of the gospel of the glory of Christ. As one who is blind, the sinner is in darkness, unable to see, and without the spiritual light that comes from beholding Christ in faith.

Keep in mind, however, that it is not the case here that man is blinded and veiled to the extent that he cannot see or come to the light of Christ (Semipelagianism). Nor is it the case that man was blinded and veiled but God provided a prevenient grace[8] so that every man can, if he wills to, cooperate and come to the light (classic Arminianism). Neither of these options is present in the text. On the contrary, God acts in a direct, unilateral, unconditional, monergistic manner, creating sight where there was *only* blindness.

As Paul says in verse 6, "For God, who said, 'Let light shine out of darkness,' has shone in our hearts to give the light of the knowledge of the glory of God in the face of Jesus Christ." Paul is referring to Genesis 1:3, where God creates light when "darkness was over the face of the deep" (Gen. 1:2). Though darkness hovered over the face of the deep, the Spirit also hovered over the face of the waters (Gen. 1:2), so that at God's very word light would be created. As Genesis 1:3–4 states,

> And God said, "Let there be light," and there was light. And God saw that the light was good. And God separated the light from the darkness.

Paul, speaking from personal experience (Acts 9:1–20), uses this language and miraculous event to describe what takes place when God transforms a sinner. Just as God calls light into being where there is only darkness, so also God calls spiritual light (the light of the glory of his own Son) into being where there is only spiritual darkness. The language of calling light out of darkness resembles the biblical language of regeneration as an act that brings about a new creation (2 Cor. 5:17; Gal. 6:15).

CONCLUSION

It has been a common practice among evangelicals to say, "you must be born again" in such a way that it is equivalent to the command to repent and trust in Christ. However, these evangelicals wrongly assume that the new birth is something we must do. In Scripture the new birth is something God accomplishes and gives to us. As seen above, the new birth is not a work conditioned on our will, but rather any spiritual activity by our will is conditioned on God's sovereign decision to grant us new life by the Spirit.

NOTES

1 John Calvin, *Institutes of the Christian Religion*, ed. John T. McNeil, trans. Ford Lewis Battles, LCC, vols. 20–21 (Philadelphia: Westminster, 1960), 2.2.16.

2 John Owen, "A Display of Arminianism," *The Works of John Owen* (Edinburgh: Banner of Truth, 2000), 10:130.

3 Anthony Hoekema, *Saved by Grace* (Grand Rapids: Eerdmans, 1989), 68. See Berkhof, *Systematic Theology*, 459–61.

4 John Owen, "A Discourse Concerning the Holy Spirit," *The Works of John Owen*, 3:318.

5 Albrecht Oepke, "Elkō," in *Theological Dictionary of the New Testament*, ed. Gerhard Kittel, ed. and trans. Geoffrey W. Bromiley (Grand Rapids: Eerdmans, 1964), 2:503.

6 Matthew Barrett, *Salvation by Grace: The Case for Effectual Calling and Regeneration* (Phillipsburg, NJ: P&R Publishing, 2013), 127.

7 Some will object, appealing to Deuteronomy 10:16, Jeremiah 4:4, and Ezekiel 18:31. For a response, see Barrett, *Salvation by Grace*, 141–44.

8. Prevenient grace is a doctrine affirmed by those in the Arminian and Wesleyan-Arminian traditions. In short, prevenient grace refers to God providing a grace that gives sinners the free-will ability to choose or reject God. Prevenient grace does not necessarily result in conversion and regeneration. Rather, it merely makes the sinner capable of choosing for himself whether he will cooperate with or resist subsequent acts of God's grace that would result in conversion and regeneration. Some Arminians believe prevenient grace is universal, while others believe it is limited to where the gospel is preached. For a fuller description and evaluation of prevenient grace, see Barrett, *Salvation by Grace*, chapters 5 and 6.

ALSO BY MATTHEW BARRETT

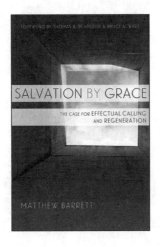

In *Salvation by Grace*, Matthew Barrett comprehensively defends the doctrine of monergism (the teaching that regeneration is exclusively the work of God) primarily by looking at Scripture but also by examining Reformed theologians and confessions. Barrett also provides a helpful evaluation of both the Arminian position and contemporary attempts to chart a middle course between Calvinistic and Arminian systems.

"Matthew Barrett's work on regeneration represents scholarship at its best. His book is exegetically convincing and theologically profound, with significant pastoral consequences."
—**Thomas R. Schreiner,** James Buchanan Harrison Professor of New Testament Interpretation, The Southern Baptist Theological Seminary, Louisville, Kentucky

ALSO BY MATTHEW BARRETT

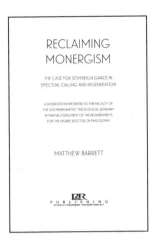

RECLAIMING
MONERGISM

THE CASE FOR SOVEREIGN GRACE IN
EFFECTUAL CALLING AND REGENERATION

A DISSERTATION PRESENTED TO THE FACULTY OF
THE SOUTHERN BAPTIST THEOLOGICAL SEMINARY
IN PARTIAL FULFILLMENT OF THE REQUIREMENTS
FOR THE DEGREE DOCTOR OF PHILOSOPHY

MATTHEW BARRETT

P U B L I S H I N G

This e-book is the original dissertation on which Matthew Barrett's book *Salvation by Grace: The Case for Effectual Calling and Regeneration* is based. It includes chapters on the history of the monergism-synergism debate; more extensive chapters representing and critiquing synergism; appendixes on the love of God, the will of God, and the relationship between effectual calling and regeneration in the Reformed tradition; as well as an extensive bibliography.

Praise for *Salvation by Grace*

"Matthew Barrett lays out the historical, theological, and biblical material and presents a compelling case for classic anti-Pelagian theology. Very helpful."

—**Carl R. Trueman,** Paul Woolley Professor of Church History, Westminster Theological Seminary, Philadelphia